USBORNE
ROUND
THE
WORLD
IN ITALIAN

First published in 1980
Usborne Publishing Ltd
20 Garrick Street
London WC2E 9BJ, England

© Usborne Publishing Ltd 1980

Printed and bound in Great Britain

About this book

This book is for everyone who is learning Italian. By looking at the pictures, it will be easy to read and learn the words underneath them.

Masculine and Feminine Words

When you look at the words in Italian, you will see that most of them have **il, lo, la, l'**, which means 'the' (singular) in front of them. When learning Italian, it is a good idea to learn the **il, lo, la** or **l'** with each word. This is because all Italian words, like house or shark, as well as woman and man, are feminine or masculine. When you see **la** the word is feminine. **Il** or **lo** means the word is masculine. **L'** is used for both masculine and feminine words in the singular beginning with a vowel.

If the word is plural — that is, there is more than one thing, such as sharks or houses, then the word has **i, gli** or **le** in front of it. **I** and **gli** are masculine, **le** is feminine.

Looking at the words

Some Italian words also have an accent on the last letter of the word. This means that the last part of the word is stressed when it is spoken.

Saying the words

At the back of the book is a guide to pronouncing all the words on the pictures. This is to help you say all the words. But there are some sounds in Italian which are quite different from any sound in English. To say them as an Italian person would say them, you have to hear them spoken. Listen very carefully and then try to say them like that yourself. But if you say them as they are written in the pronunciation guide, an Italian person will understand you — even if your Italian accent is not quite perfect.

Can you find the dog?

On every picture across two pages there is a spotty dog to look for. Can you find it?

With Easy Pronunciation Guide

Carol Watson and Mariolina Freeth
Illustrated by David Mostyn

Pronunciation guide by Anne Becker

In città

la chiesa

l'autorimessa

la casa

il parco

la fermata dell'autobus

il semaforo

il passaggio pedonale

il cartellone pubblicitario

il segnale stradale

l'albergo

la fabbrica

il negozio

la ciminiera

il cameriere

la caserma dei pompieri

la macchina dei pompieri

4

gli appartamenti

il campo-giochi

il balcone

l'ospedale

la statua

il banco dei fiori

il postino

l'edicola
dei giornali

l'auto della polizia
il lampione

la strada
sopraelevata

l'antenna

il marciapiede

l'ombrellone

il caffè

il cinema

5

In viaggio !

il treno

il risciò

il biplano

il furgoncino

la bicicletta

il furgone per cavalli

la carretta

il pallone aerostatico

la macchina sportiva

l'autobus

l'autotreno per auto

l'autocisterna

il deltaplano

la monorotaia

il carro armato

il carrello portabaga

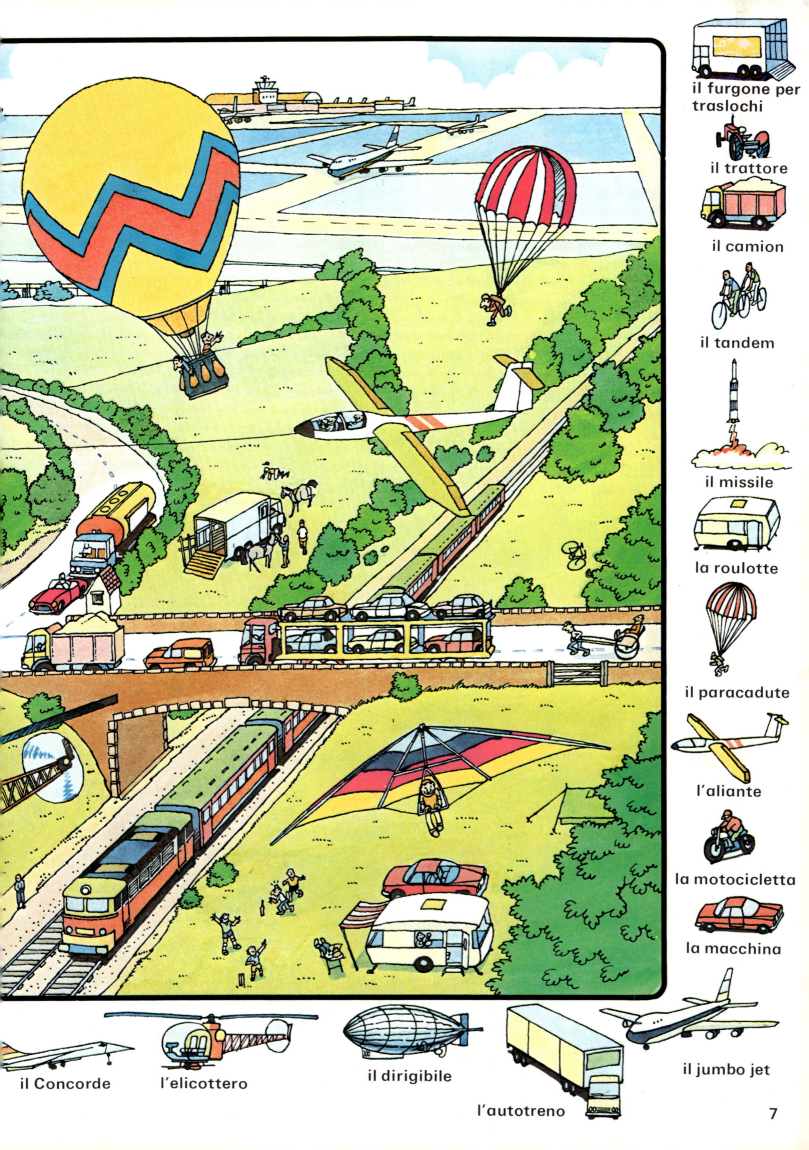

il furgone per traslochi

il trattore

il camion

il tandem

il missile

la roulotte

il paracadute

l'aliante

la motocicletta

la macchina

il jumbo jet

il Concorde

l'elicottero

il dirigibile

l'autotreno

7

Sull' acqua

la rete da pesca

il cestino da picnic

il fiume

lo sbarramento

il canale

le code-di-cavallo

la canoa

il ponte

la canna da pesca

la lenza

il pescatore

la sedia a sdraio

la chiatta

l'anatra

l'anatroccolo

l'acquedotto

8

la zattera

la chiusa

il motoscafo

il motore di fuoribordo

il canotto di gomma

il pontile

la darsena coperta

i giunchi

la casa galleggiante

la pagaia

il galleggiante

il motoscafo cabinato

il cigno

la barca a remi

il remo

9

Nel porto

il rimorchiatore

l'hovercraft

la gru

la bitta

il deposito merci

la boa

i sacchi

la cassetta

l'oblò

il sottomarino

lo scaricatore

la chiatta

il fumaiolo

la nave traghetto

il cassone

la bandiera

10

il peschereccio

il pescatore

l'uncino

l'áncora

l'aliscafo

la cisterna

la rete

il marinaio

la scaletta

la vela

la petroliera

il piroscafo

la cassa da imballaggio

la scialuppa de salvataggio

la draga

il salvagente

la barca a vela

11

In montagna

la roccia

lo scalatore

la corda

il muflone

la capra selvatica

l'aquila

il picco

la piccozza

il ghiacciaio

il puma

i sassi

gli sci

l'abete

la caverna

la cartina

l'escursionista

12

la sciovia

il masso

lo zaino

la cascata

l'orso l'orsacchiotto

le corna

l'alce

la capanna di legno

la foresta

il boscaiolo

il binocolo

il tronco

la sega

gli scarponi da montagna

la scure

13

Nel deserto

l'asino

la sella

il topo saltatore

il nomade

il cammello

la volpe del deserto

il pozzo petrolifero

lo struzzo

l'antilope

il falco

la sabbia

la duna

il cespuglio

il pozzo

la tartaruga del deserto

la gazzella

la jeep

la palma

la groppiera

il teschio

lo scheletro

il serpente

la lepre

l'avvoltoio

il giglio
del deserto

l'ormica

la tenda

l'oasi

la lucertola

lo scorpione

Sotto il mare

il pescecane

la pinna del pesce

il pesce

la maschera

le bombole

la sabbia

i sassolini

la spugna

lo scoglio

16

il relitto

il forziere

la fune

la grotta

la stella marina

il granchio

l'aragosta

la conchiglia

le alghe

l'ostrica

l'anemone di mare

il cavalluccio marino

la bollicina

il polipo

il tentacolo

la medusa

la pinna del sub

la muta

il subacqueo

17

il gorilla

il bambù

il rampicante

il tucano

il ragno

la freccia

il cacciatore

la raganella

la farfalla

Nella giungla

18 la canoa

lo scienziato

il fungo

il giaguaro

lo scimpanzè

il camaleonte

il serpente

il pipistrello

il tapiro

la scimmia

il coccodrillo

il lori

il bradipo

il pappagallo

le impronte

rchidea

il colibrì

il tronco dell'albero

la foglia

il ponte di corda

il formichiere

19

Paesi freddi

l'iceberg

il ghiaccio

il cane da slitta

il cappuccio

l'arpione

gli occhiali da neve

il ghiacciolo

il pupazzo di neve

la palla di neve

l'igloo

l'aereo con i pattini

il rompighiaccio

la rondine marina

la foca

il kayak

20

la renna

il tricheco

l'orso polare

la neve

il trattore da neve

la slitta

la balena

la volpe bianca

il gatto delle nevi

il gufo bianco

le racchette da neve

i guantoni

la motoslitta

l'Eschimese

21

lo scudo

il tamburo

il falò

il cerchio

l'acrobata

la strega

il giocoliere

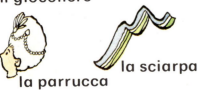
la parrucca

A carnevale

la sciarpa

lo stendardo

la nappa

il pennacchio

la maschera

il mantello

l'elmo

la lanterna

i fuochi d'artificio

la danzatrice

i trampoli

il manico di scopa

il pagliaccio

l'orecchino

il baldacchino

la piuma

i palloncini

gli speroni

la fiamma

la candela

la lancia

la bandierina

la carrozza

23

La musica

il corno

il timpano

le bacchette dei tamburi

le nacchere

il tamburello

l'oboe

il triangolo

la chitarra elettrica

il leggìo

il direttore d'orchestra

l'organo

la cetra indiana

la fisarmonica

la fisarmonichetta

il silofono

il fagotto

la tromba

l'armonica a bocca

il violoncello

la tuba

la balalaika

il violino

l'archetto

il sassofono

i piatti

l'arpa

il flauto dolce

le maracas

il campanello

la chitarra

il clarinetto

cornamusa

il trombone

il bangio

il flauto

il contrabbasso

il pianoforte

25

Da mangiare e da bere

lo spiedino alla brace

le frittelle

l'hot-dog

il tacchino

la pesca

le ostriche

le patatine fritte

la mela

il gelato

i würster

gli spaghetti

la prugna

l'hamburger

il pane

il latte

il pomodoro

il caffè

le fragole

la birra

il tramezzino

il formaggio

il pesce

il pasticcio
di carne

il tè

il vino

la torta

il budino
di gelatina

la pera

le ciliegie

la limonata

le lumache

la pannocchia di
granturco

il riso

l'insalata

il gonnellino
di paglia

gli stivali

il chimono

i jeans

la farfalla

il caffettano

il berretto

la tonaca del prete

il basco

Come ci vestiamo

la
mantellina

la bombetta

il bolero

le pantofole

lo scialle

il cappello
da cow-boy   la cuf

la tuta sportiva

il cilindro

il poncio

il gonnellino
scozzese

il sombrero

il sari

il fez

il velo
mussulmano

tonaca
ella monaca

il frac

il turbante

i gambali

i sandali

lo smoking

il cappello di
paglia cinese

gli zoccoli
olandesi

la tuta
spaziale

29

I raccolti

il tabacco

il riso

i datteri

il grano

i cavoli

le noci di cocco

i tulipani

il cotone

l'uva

il cacao

il tè

gli ananas

i girasoli

il caffè

la canna da zucchero

le banane

il legname

31

I pericoli della natura

l'iceberg

le sabbie mobili

l'onda di maremoto

il vulcano

il terremoto

32

il ciclone

la tromba marina

l'incendio nella foresta

la valanga

il fulmine

la tormenta

la tromba d'aria

la tempesta di sabbia

l'inondazione

33

Dove abita la gente

la tenda beduina

la capanna di fango secco

il villino inglese

la casetta sull'albero

la tenda indiana

il capannone del Borneo

la casa galleggiante

la tenda mongola

la chiatta da canale

la casa sperimentale a cupola

la capanna di stuoia

la capanna di giunchi

lo chalet svizzero

gli appartamenti

il ranch sudamericano

la casa di carta giapponese

la fattoria spagnola

il faro

il carrozzone degli zingari

le case scavate nel tufo

la casetta di campagna

la casa su palafitte

il castello tedesco

il forte americano

la capanna di legno

il sampan cinese

le case inglesi a terrazza

35

Gli animali

l'orango

il bisonte

il vombato

il koala

l'uistitì

il leone

il castoro

il bue muschiato

la testuggine gigante

l'ippopotamo

l'orsetto lavatore

la zebra

il delfino

il tasso

l'elefante

la marmotta striata

il gibbone

il panda gigante

il lama

la tigre

la puzzola

lo gnu

il lemure

il porcospino

l'armadillo

la iena

il babbuino

il canguro

la giraffa

il lupo

il leopardo

il rinoceronte

Monumenti e posti famosi

1 Il Castello di Ludovico
   – Germania

2 Il Golden Gate di San Francisco
   – Stati Uniti

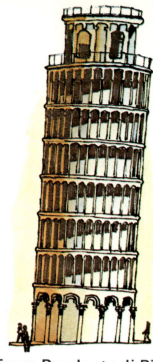

3 La Torre Pendente di Pis
   –Italia

4 La Moschea Azzurra
   – Iran

5 L'Opera di Sydney
   –Australia

7 Il Monte Everest
   – Nepal

6 Le Cascate del Niagara
   – Stati Uniti e Canadà

8 La Torre Eiffel
   – Francia

9 Stonehenge
   –Inghilterra

10 La Cattedrale di San Basilio
   – Russia

11   Il Taj Mahal
     – India

12   La Sfinge e una piramide
     – Egitto

13   Il Gran Canyon
     – Stati Uniti

14   La Torre di Londra
     – Inghilterra

15   Il Partenone
     – Grecia

16   La Statua della Libertà
     – Stati Uniti

17   Il Colosseo
     – Italia

18   Cape Kennedy
     – Stati Uniti

19   Il Tempio del Paradiso
     – Cina

Look at the map on the next two pages. Match up the numbers to find out where the buildings and places are in the world.

Il mondo

LA GROENLANDIA

l'igloo

L'OCEANO ARTICO

il peschereccio

L'ALASCA

l'Esquimese

l'hovercraft

L'EUROPA

IL CANADÀ

6

16

GLI STATI UNITI D'AMERICA

il missile

18

il Concorde

L'OCEANO ATLANTICO

L'AFRICA

13

2

il piroscafo

IL SUD AMERICA

L'OCEANO PACIFICO

9 14

8

1

3

Can you name the animals?

la barca a vela

You can find them in this book.

40

The numbers on the map show where the famous buildings and places are to be found. See pages 38 and 39.

il pallone aerostatico

LA RUSSIA

L'OCEANO PACIFICO

l'onda di maremoto

19

LA CINA

il sottomarino

4

7

11

il pozzo petrolifero

L'INDIA

la petroliera

il jumbo jet

L'AUSTRALIA

il rompighiaccio

LA NUOVA ZELANDA

l'elicottero

L'ANTARTIDE

il gatto delle nevi

41

Index

On this page is the start of the alphabetical list of all the words in the pictures in this book. The Italian word comes first, then there is its pronunciation in *italics*, followed by the English translation.

There are some sounds in the Italian language which are quite different from any sounds in English. The pronunciation is a guide to help you say the Italian words correctly. They may look funny or strange. Just read them as if they are English words, except for these special rules:

ay — is like the *a* in *date*
o — is like the *o* in *hot*
ow — is like the *ow* in *cow*
e — is like the *e* in *ten* even when followed by *r* — so *per* sounds like *pear* not like the *per* in *proper*
ly — sounds like the *lli* in *brilliant*
ny — sounds like the *ni* in *onion*
r — is always pronounced — sounded — never missed out
g — is like the *g* in *get*
s — is always said like the *s* in *set*

Italian	Pronunciation	English
l'abete (m)	*la-bay-tay*	fir tree
abitare	*a-beet-a-ray*	to live
l'acquedotto (m)	*lack-kway-dot-to*	aqueduct
l'acrobata (m)	*la-cro-ba-ta*	acrobat
l'aereo con i pattini (m)	*la-ay-ray-o con ee pat-tee-nee*	ski plane
l'Africa (f)	*la-free-ca*	Africa
l'Alasca (f)	*la-lass-ca*	Alaska
l'albergo (m)	*lal-ber-go*	hotel
l'alce (m)	*lal-chay*	moose
le alghe (f)	*lay al-gay*	seaweed
l'aliante (m)	*lal-ee-an-tay*	glider
l'aliscafo (m)	*lal-ee-sca-fo*	hydrofoil
americano	*a-may-ree-ca-no*	American
l'ananas (m)	*la-na-nass*	pineapple
l'anatra (f)	*la-na-tra*	duck
l'anatroccolo (m)	*la-na-trock-co-lo*	duckling
l'ancora (f)	*lan-co-ra*	anchor
gli animali (m)	*lyee a-nee-ma-lee*	animals
l'Antartide (f)	*lan-tar-tee-day*	Antarctica
l'antenna (f)	*lan-ten-na*	aerial
l'antilope (f)	*lan-tee-lo-pay*	antelope
gli appartamenti (m)	*lyee ap-par-ta-men-tee*	flats
l'appartamento (m)	*lap-par-ta-men-to*	flat
l'aquila (f)	*la-kwee-la*	eagle
l'aragosta (f)	*la-ra-goss-ta*	lobster
l'archetto (m)	*lar-ket-to*	bow (violin)
l'armadillo (m)	*lar-ma-deel-lo*	armadillo
l'armonica a bocca (f)	*lar-mo-nee-ca a bock-ca*	harmonica
l'arpa (f)	*lar-pa*	harp
l'arpione (m)	*lar-pee-o-nay*	harpoon
l'asino (m)	*la-see-no*	donkey
l'attinia (f)	*lat-tee-nee-a*	sea anemone
l'Australia (f)	*low-stra-lee-a*	Australia
l'auto della polizia (f)	*low-to del-la po-lee-tsee-a*	police car
l'autobus (m)	*low-to-booce*	bus
l'autocisterna (f)	*low-to-chee-ster-na*	petrol tanker
l'autotrano (m)	*low-to-tray-no*	juggernaut
l'avvoltoio (m)	*lav-vol-toy-o*	vulture
il babbuino	*eel ba-boo-ee-no*	baboon
le bacchette dei tamburi (f)	*lay back-ket-tay day-ee tam-boo-ree*	drumsticks
la balalaika	*la ba-la-la-ee-ca*	balalaika
il balcone	*eel bal-co-nay*	balcony
il baldaccino	*eel bal-dach-chee-no*	canopy
la balena	*la ba-lay-na*	whale
il bambù	*eel bam-boo*	bamboo
le banane (f)	*lay ba-na-nay*	bananas
il banco dei fiori	*eel ban-co day-ee fee-or-ee*	flower stall
la bandiera	*la ban-dee-ay-ra*	flag
la bandierina	*la ban-dee-ay-ree-na*	banner
il bangio	*eel ban-jo*	banjo
la barca a remi	*la bar-ca a ray-mee*	rowing boat
la barca a vela	*la bar-ca a vay-la*	dinghy
il basco	*eel ba-sco*	beret
beduina	*bay-doo-ee-na*	Bedouin (adj)
il berretto	*eel bay-rayt-to*	cap
la bicicletta	*la bee-chee-clet-ta*	bicycle
il binocolo	*eel bee-no-co-lo*	binoculars
il biplano	*eel bee-pla-no*	bi-plane
la birra	*la beer-ra*	beer
la bisarca	*la bee-zar-ca*	transporter
il bisonte	*eel bee-zon-tay*	bison
la bitta	*la beet-ta*	bollard
la boa	*la bo-a*	buoy
il bolero	*eel bo-lay-ro*	bolero
la bollicina	*la bol-lee-chee-na*	bubble
la bombetta	*la bom-bet-ta*	bowler hat
le bombole	*lay bom-bo-lay*	aqualung
il boscaiolo	*eel boss-ca-ee-o-lo*	lumberjack

il bradipo	*eel bra-dee-po*	sloth
il budino di gelatina	*eel boo-dee-no dee jel-a-tee-na*	jelly
il bue muschiato	*eel boo-ay moo-scee-a-to*	yak
il bungalow inglese	*eel boon-ga-lo een-glay-zay*	bungalow
il cacao	*eel ca-ca-o*	cocoa
il cacciatore	*eel cach-cha-to-ray*	hunter
il caffè	*eel caf-fay*	café, coffee
il caffettano	*eel caf-fet-ta-no*	kaftan
il camaleonte	*eel ca-ma-lay-on-tay*	chameleon
il cameriere	*eel ca-may-ree-ay-ray*	waiter
il camion	*eel ca-mee-on*	lorry
il cammello	*eel cam-mel-lo*	camel
il campanello	*eel cam-pa-nel-lo*	handbell
il campo giochi	*eel cam-po jo-kee*	playground
il Canada	*eel ca-na-da*	Canada
il canale	*eel ca-na-lay*	canal
la candela	*la can-day-la*	candle
il cane da slitta	*eel ca-nay da sleet-ta*	husky dog
il canguro	*eel can-goo-ro*	kangaroo
la canna da pesca	*la can-na da pess-ca*	rod
la canna da zucchero	*la can-na da tsoo-kay-ro*	sugar cane
la canoa	*la ca-no-a*	canoe
il canotto di gomma	*eel ca-not-to dee gom-ma*	rubber dinghy
la capanna	*la ca-pan-na*	hut, cabin
la capanna di fango secco	*la ca-pan-na dee fan-go seck-co*	mud hut
la capanna di giunchi	*la ca-pan-na dee joon-kee*	reed house
la capanna di legno	*la ca-pan-na dee lay-nyo*	log cabin
la capanna di stuoia	*la ca-pan-na dee stoo-o-ya*	grass hut
il capannone del Borneo	*eel ca-pan-no-nay del bor-nay-o*	long house
Cape Kennedy	*cape-ken-nay-dee*	Cape Kennedy
il cappello da cowboy	*eel cap-pel-lo da cow-boy*	stetson
il cappello di paglia cinese	*eel cap-pel-lo dee pa-lyee-a chee-nay-zay*	coolie hat
il cappuccio	*eel cap-pooch-cho*	hood
la capra selvatica	*la ca-pra sell-va-tee-ca*	mountain goat
il carnevale	*eel car-nay-va-lay*	carnival
a Carnevale	*a car-nay-va-lay*	at the carnival
la carretta	*la car-ret-ta*	horse and cart
il carro armato	*eel car-ro ar-ma-to*	tank
la carrozza	*la car-rot-sa*	carriage
il carrozzone degli zingari	*eel car-rot-so-nay day lyee dzeen-ga-ree*	gypsy caravan
il cartellone pubblicitario	*eel car-tell-lo-nay poob-blee-chee-ta-ree-o*	advertisement
la cartina	*la car-tee-na*	map
la casa	*la ca-za*	house
la casa di carta giapponese	*la ca-za dee car-ta jap-pon-ay-zay*	paper house
la casa galleggiante	*la ca-za gal-lej-jee-an-tay*	houseboat
la casa sperimantale a cupola	*la caza spay-ree-man-ta-lay a coo-po-la*	dome house
la casa su palafitte	*la ca-za soo pa-la-feet-tay*	stilt house
la cascata	*la cass-ca-ta*	waterfall
le Cascate del Niagara	*lay cas-ca-tay dell nee-a-ga-ra*	Niagara Falls
le case inglesi a terrazza	*lay ca-zay een-glay-zee a ter-rat-za*	terraced house
le case scavate nel tufo	*lay ca-zay sca-va-tay nell too-fo*	cave house
la caserma dei pompieri	*la ca-zer-ma day-ee pom-pee-ay-ree*	fire station
la casetta sull' albero	*la ca-zet-ta sool lal-bay-ro*	tree house
la cassa da imballaggio	*la cas-sa da eem-bal-laj-jo*	crate
la cassetta	*la cas-se-ta*	box
il cassone	*eel cas-so-nay*	container
il Castello di Ludovico	*eel cas-tell-lo dee loo-do-vee-co*	Ludwig's Castle
il castello tedesco	*eel cas-tell-lo tay-des-co*	castle
il castoro	*eel cas-to-ro*	beaver
la Cattedrale di San Basilio	*la cat-tay-dra-lay dee san ba-zee-lee-o*	St Basil's Cathedral
il cavalluccio marino	*eel ca-val-looch-cho ma-ree-no*	sea horse
la caverna	*la ca-ver-na*	cave
i cavoli	*ee ca-vo-lee*	cabbages
il cavolo	*eel ca-vo-lo*	cabbage
il cerchio	*eel cher-kee-o*	hoop
il cestino da picnic	*eel ches-tee-no da peek-neek*	hamper (picnic)
la cetra indiana	*la chay-tra een-dee-a-na*	sitar
lo chalet svizzero	*lo sha-lay svit-say-ro*	chalet
la chiatta	*la kee-at-ta*	barge
la chiatta da canale	*la kee-at-ta da ca-na-lay*	canal barge
la chiesa	*la kee-ay-za*	church
il chimono	*eel kee-mo-no*	kimono
la chitarra	*la kee-tar-ra*	guitar
la chitarra elettrica	*la kee-tar-ra ay-let-tree-ca*	electric guitar
la chiusa	*la kee-oo-za*	lockgates
il ciclone	*eel chee-clo-nay*	hurricane
il cigno	*eel chee-nyo*	swan
la ciliegia	*la chee-lee-ay-ja*	cherry
le ciliegie	*lay chee-lee-ay-jee*	cherries
il cilindro	*eel chee-leen-dro*	top hat
la ciminiera	*la chee-mee-nee-ay-ra*	chimney
la Cina	*la chee-na*	China
il cinema	*eel chee-nay-ma*	cinema
cinese	*chee-nay-zay*	Chinese
la cisterna	*la cheest-er-na*	storage tank
il clarinetto	*eel cla-ree-net-to*	clarinet
il clown	*eel clown*	clown
il coccodrillo	*eel cock-cod-reel-lo*	crocodile
le code-di-cavallo (f)	*lay co-day-dee-ca-val-lo*	bulrushes

il colibri	eel co-lee-bree	humming bird
il Colosseo	eel co-los-say-o	Colosseum
come ci vestiamo	co-may chee vest-ee-a-mo	the way we dress
la conchiglia	la con-kee-lyee-a	shell
il Concorde	eel con-cord	Concorde
il contrabbasso	eel con-trab-bas-so	double bass
la corda	la cor-da	rope
le corna (f)	lay cor-na	antlers
la cornamusa (f)	la cor-na-moo-za	bagpipes
il corno	eel cor-no	French horn
il cotone	eel co-to-nay	cotton
il cottage	eel cot-ta-jay	cottage
la cuffia	la coof-fee-a	bonnet
la danzatrice	la dant-za-tree-chay	dancer (female)
la darsena coperta	la dar-say-na co-per-ta	boathouse
i datteri (m)	ee dat-tay-ree	dates (fruit)
il delfino	eel del-fee-no	dolphin
il deltaplano	eel del-ta pla-no	hang glider
il deposito merci	eel day-po-zee-to merchee	warehouse
il deserto	eel day-zer-to	desert
il direttore d'orchestra	eel dee-ret-to-ray dor-kes-tra	conductor
il dirigibile	eel dee-ree-jee-bee-lay	airship
dolce	dol-chay	sweet
dove	do-vay	where
dove abita la gente	do-vay a-bee-ta la jen-tay	where people live
la draga	la dra-ga	dredger
la duna	la doo-na	dune
l'edicola dei giornali (f)	lay-dee-co-la day-ee jor-na-lee	newspaper stand
l'Egitto (m)	lay-jeet-to	Egypt
l'elephante (m)	lay-lay-fan-tay	elephant
l'elicottero (m)	lay-lee-cot-tay-ro	helicopter
l'elmo (m)	lel-mo	helmet
l'escursionista (m)	less-coor-see-on-ee-sta	walker
l'Esquimese (m)	les-kwee-may-zay	Eskimo
l'Europa (f)	lay-oo-ro-pa	Europe
la fabbrica	la fab-bree-ca	factory
il fagotto	eel fa-got-to	bassoon
il falco	eel fal-co	hawk
il falo	eel fa-lo	bonfire
la farfalla	la far-fal-la	butterfly
il faro	eel fa-ro	lighthouse
la fattoria spagnola	la fat-to-ree-a spa-nyo-la	farmhouse
la fermata dell' autobus	la fer-ma-ta del low-to-booce	bus stop
il fez	eel fez	fez
la fiamma	la fee-am-ma	flame
la fisarmonica	la fee-zar-mo-nee-ca	accordion
la fisarmonichetta	la fee-zar-mo-nee-ket-ta	concertina
il fiume	eel fee-oo-may	river
il flauto	eel flow-to	flute
il flauto dolce	eel flow-to dol-chay	recorder
la foca	la fo-ca	seal
la foglia	la fo-lyee-a	leaf

la foresta	la fo-res-ta	forest
il formaggio	eel for-maj-jo	cheese
la formica	la for-mee-ca	ant
il formichiere	eel for-mee-kee-ay-ray	anteater
il forte americano	eel for-tay a-may-ree-ca-no	fort
il forziere	eel for-tsee-ay-ray	treasure chest
il frac	eel frak	tailcoat
le fragole (f)	lay fra-go-lay	strawberries
la Francia	la fran-cha	France
la freccia	la frech-cha	arrow
freddo	fred-do	cold
la frittella	la freet-tel-la	pancake
il fulmine	eel fool-mee-nay	lightning
il fumaiolo	eel foo-ma-yo-lo	funnel
la fune	la foo-nay	rope
il fungo	eel foon-go	mushroom
i fuochi d'artificio (m)	ee foo-o-kee dar-tee-fee-cho	fireworks
il fuoribordo	eel foo-o-ree-bor-do	outboard motor
il furgone	eel foor-go-nay	van
il furgone per cavalli	eel foor-go-nay per ca-val-lee	horse box
il furgone per traslochi	eel foor-go-nay per tra zlo-kee	removal van
il galleggiante	eel gal-layj-jan-tay	float
i gambali (m)	ee gam-ba-lee	chaps
il garage	eel ga-raj	garage
il gatto delle nevi	eel gat-to del-lay nay-vee	snow cat
la gazzella	la gad-zel-la	gazelle
il gelato	eel jay-la-to	ice cream
la gente	la jen-tay	people
Germania	jer-man-ee-a	Germany
il ghiacciaio	eel gee-ach-cha-yo	glacier
il ghiaccio	eel gee-ach-cho	ice
il ghiacciolo	eel gee-ach-cho-lo	icicle
il giaguaro	eel jee-a-gwa-ro	jaguar
giapponese	jap-po-nay-zay	Japanese
il gibbone	eel jeeb-bo-nay	gibbon
il giglio del deserto	eel jee-lyee-o del day-zer-to	desert lily
il giocoliere	eel jo-co-lee-ay-ray	juggler
la giraffa	la jee-raf-fa	giraffe
il girasole	eel jee-ra-so-lay	sunflower
i giunchi (m)	ee joon-kee	reeds
la giungla	la joon-gla	jungle
lo gnu	lo nyoo	gnu
il Golden Gate di San Francisco	eel gol-den gayt dee san fran-chees-co	The Golden Gate Bridge
il gonnellino di paglia	eel gon-nel-lee-no dee pa-lyee-a	grass skirt
il gonnellino scozzese	eel gon-nel-lee-no scot-say-zay	kilt
il gorilla	eel go-reel-la	gorilla
il Gran Canyon	eel gran-can-yon	Grand Canyon
il granchio	eel gran-kee-o	crab
il grano	eel grano	wheat
la Grecia	la gre-cha	Greece
la Groenlandia	la gro-en-lan-dee-a	Greenland
la groppiera	la grop-pee-ay-ra	blanket
la grotta	la grot-ta	cave

la gru	*la groo*	crane
i guantoni (m)	*ee gwan-to-nee*	mittens
il gufo bianco	*eel goo-fo bee-an-co*	snowy owl
l'hamburger	*lam-boor-ger*	hamburger
l'hot-dog (m)	*lot-dog*	hotdog
l'hovercraft	*lo-ver-craft*	hovercraft
l'iceberg (m)	*liez-berg*	iceberg
la iena	*la yay-na*	hyena
l'igloo (m)	*lee-gloo*	igloo
le impronte (f)	*lay eem-pron-tay*	tracks
l'incendio nella foresta (m)	*leen-chen-dee-o nel-la fo-res-ta*	forest fire
in città	*een-chee-ta*	in the city
in fondo al mare	*een fon-do al ma-ray*	at the bottom of the sea
l'India (f)	*leen-dee-a*	India
l'Inghilterra (f)	*leen-geel-ter-ra*	England
inglese/inglesi (adj.)	*een-glay-zay/een-glay-zee*	English
l'inondazione (f)	*leen-on-da-tsee-o-nay*	flood
l'insalata (f)	*leen-sa-la-ta*	salad
l'ippopotamo (m)	*leep-po-po-ta-mo*	hippopotamus
l'Iran (m)	*lee-ran*	Iran
l'Italia (f)	*lee-ta-lee-a*	Italy
i jeans	*ee jeens*	jeans
la jeep	*la jeep*	jeep
il jumbo jet	*eel joom-bo jet*	jumbo jet
il kayak	*eel ca-yak*	kayak
il koala	*eel ko-a-la*	koala bear
il lama	*eel la-ma*	llama
il lampione	*eel lam-pee-o-nay*	lamp post
la lancia	*la lan-cha*	spear
la lanterna	*la lan-ter-na*	lantern
il latte	*eel lat-tay*	milk
il leggio	*eel lej-jo*	music stand
il legname	*eel lay-nya-may*	timber
il legno	*eel lay-nyo*	wood
il lemure	*eel lay-moo-ray*	lemur
la lenza	*la lent-za*	fishing line
il leone	*eel lay-o-nay*	lion
il leopardo	*eel lay-o-par-do*	leopard
la lepre	*la lay-pray*	hare
la limonata	*la lee-mo-na-ta*	lemonade
il lori	*eel lo-ree*	bushbaby
la lucertola	*la loo-cher-to-la*	lizard
le lumache (f)	*lay loo-ma-kay*	snails
il lupo	*eel loo-po*	wolf
la macchina	*la mack-kee-na*	car
la macchina dei pompieri	*la mack-kee-na day-ee pom-pee-ay-ree*	fire engine
la macchina sportiva	*la mack-kee-na spor-tee-va*	sports car
da mangiare e da bere	*da man-jar-ay ay da bay-ray*	food and drink
il manico di scopa	*eel ma-nee-co dee sco-pa*	broomstick
la mantellina	*la man-tel-lee-na*	cape
il mantello	*eel man-tel-lo*	cloak

le maracas (f)	*lay ma-ra-cas*	maracas
il marciapiede	*eel mar-cha-pee-ay-day*	pavement
il mare	*eel ma-ray*	sea
il marinaio	*eel ma-ree-na-yo*	sailor
la marmotta striata	*la mar-mot-ta stree-a-ta*	chipmunk
la maschera	*la mas-kay-ra*	mask
il masso	*eel mas-so*	boulder
la medusa	*la may-doo-za*	jellyfish
la mela	*la may-la*	apple
il missile	*eel mees-see-lay*	rocket
la monaca	*la mo-na-ca*	nun
il mondo	*eel mon-do*	world
la monorotaia	*la mo-no-ro-ta-ya*	monorail
in montagna	*een mon-ta-nya*	up the mountains
il Monte Everest	*eel mon-tay ay-vay-rest*	Mount Everest
la Moschea Azzurra	*la mos-kay-a ad-zoor-ra*	The Blue Mosque
la motocicletta	*la mo-to-chee-clet-ta*	motorcycle
il motore	*eel mo-to-ray*	motor
il motoscafo	*eel mo-to-sca-fo*	motorboat
il motoscafo cabinato	*eel mo-to-sca-fo ca-bee-na-to*	cabin cruiser
la motoslitta	*la mo-to sleet-ta*	snowmobile
il muflone	*eel moo-flo-nay*	mountain sheep
la muta	*la moo-ta*	wetsuit
le nacchere (f)	*lay nach-chay-ray*	castanets
la nappa	*la nap-pa*	tassel
la nave traghetto	*la na-vay tra-get-to*	ferry boat
il negozio	*eel nay-go-tsee-o*	shop
nella giungla	*nel-la joon-gla*	in the jungle
Nepal	*nay-pal*	Nepal
la neve	*la nay-vay*	snow
la noce di cocco	*la no-chay dee cock-co*	coconut
il nomade	*eel no-ma-day*	nomad
la Nuova Zelanda	*la noo-o-va tsay-lan-da*	New Zealand
l'oasi (f)	*lo-a-zee*	oasis
l'oblò (m)	*lo-blo*	porthole
l'oboe	*lo-bo-ay*	oboe
gli occhiali da neve (m)	*lyee ock-kee-a-lee da nay-vay*	goggles
l'Oceano Artico (m)	*lo-chay-a-no ar-tee-co*	Arctic Ocean
l'Oceano Atlantico (m)	*lo-chay-a-no at-lan-tee-co*	Atlantic Ocean
l'Oceano Pacifico (m)	*lo-chay-a-no pa-chee-fee-co*	Pacific Ocean
l'ombrellone (m)	*lom-brel-lo-nay*	umbrella
l'onda di maremoto (f)	*lon-da dee ma-ray-mo-to*	tidal wave
l'Opera di Sydney	*lo-pay-ra dee seed-nay*	Sydney Opera House
l'orango (m)	*lo-ran-go*	orang-utan
l'orchidea (f)	*lor-kee-day-a*	orchid
l'orecchino (m)	*lo-reck-kee-no*	earring
l'organo (m)	*lor-gan-no*	organ
l'orsacchiotto (m)	*lor-sack-kee-ot-to*	bear cub
l'orsetto lavatore (m)	*lor-set-to la-va-to-ray*	racoon

Italian	Pronunciation	English
l'orso (m)	lor-so	bear
l'orso bruno (m)	lor-so broo-no	brown bear
l'orso polare (m)	lor-so po-la-ray	polar bear
l'ospedale (m)	los-pay-da-lay	hospital
l'ostrica (f)	los-tree-ca	oyster
le ostriche	lay os-tree-cay	oysters
Paesi freddi (m)	pa-ay-zee fred-dee	cold lands
la pagaia	la pa-ga-ya	paddle
la palla di neve	la pal-la dee nay-vay	snowball
i palloncini	ee pal-lon-chee-nee	balloons
il pallone aerostatico	eel pal-lo-nay a-ay-ros-ta-tee-co	hot air balloon
la palma	la pal-ma	palm tree
il panda gigante	eel pan-da jee-gan-tay	giant panda
il pane	eel pa-nay	bread
la pannocchia di granturco	la pan-nock-kee-a dee gran-toor-co	corn
le pantofole (f)	lay pan-to-fo-lay	slippers
il pappagallo	eel pap-pa-gal-lo	parrot
il paracadute	eel pa-ra-ca-doo-tay	parachute
il parco	eel par-co	park
la parrucca	la par-rook-ca	wig
il Partenone	eel par-tay-no-nay	Parthenon
il passaggio pedonale	eel pas-saj-jo pay-do-na-lay	pedestrian crossing
le patatine fritte	lay pa-ta-tee-nay free-tay	chips
il pennacchio	eel pen-nack-kee-o	plume
la pera	la pay-ra	pear
i pericoli (m)	ee pay-ree-co-lee	dangers
la pesca	la pes-ca	peach
il pescatore	eel pes-ca-to-ray	fisherman
il pesce	eel pay-shay	fish
il pescecane	eel pay-shay-ca-nay	shark
il peschereccio	eel pes-cay-rech-cho	fishing boat
la petroliera	la pay-tro-lee-ay-ra	petrol tanker
il pianoforte	eel pee-a-no-for-tay	piano
i piatti (m)	ee pee-a-tee	cymbals
il picco	eel peek-ko	peak
la piccozza	la peek-kot-sa	ice axe
la pinna del pesce	la peen-na del pay-shay	fin
la pinna del sub	la peen-na del soob	flippers
il pipistrello	la pee-pee-strel-lo	bat
la piramide	la pee-ra-mee-day	pyramid
il piroscafo	eel pee-ro-sca-fo	liner
la piuma	la pee-oo-ma	feather
il polipo	eel po-lee-po	octopus
il pomodoro	eel po-mo-do-ro	tomato
il poncio	eel pon-cho	poncho
il ponte	eel pon-tay	bridge
il ponte di corda	eel pon-tay dee cor-da	rope bridge
il pontile	eel pon-tee-lay	jetty
il porcospino	eel por-co-spee-no	porcupine
il porto	eel por-to	port/harbour
al porto	al por-to	in the harbour
i posti famosi	ee pos-tee fa-mo-zee	famous places
il postino	eel po-stee-no	postman
il pozzo	eel pot-so	well (water)
il pozzo petrolifero	eel pot-so pay-tro-lee-fay-ro	oil well
la prugna	la proo-nya	plum
il puma	eel poo-ma	mountain lion
il pupazzo di neve	eel poo-pat-so dee nay-vay	snowman
la puzzola	la poot-so-la	skunk
le racchette da neve (f)	lay rack-ket-tay da nay-vay	snow shoes
i raccolti (m)	ee rack-col-tee	crops
la raganella	la ra-ga-nel-la	tree frog
il ragno	eel ra-nyo	spider
il rampicante	eel ram-pee-can-tay	creeper
il ranch sudamericano	eel-ransh sood-a-may-ree-ca-no	ranch
il relitto	eel ray-leet-to	wreck
il remo	eel ray-mo	oar
la renna	la ren-na	reindeer
la rete	la ray-tay	net
la rete da pesca	la ray-tay da pess-ca	fishing net
il rimorchiatore	eel ree-mor-kee-a-to-ray	tug (boat)
il rimorchio	eel ree-mor-kee-o	trailer
il rinoceronte	eel ree-no-chay-ron-tay	rhinoceros
il risciò	eel ree-sho	rickshaw
il riso	eel ree-zo	rice
la roccia	la roch-cha	rock
il rompighiaccio	eel rom-pee-gee-ach-cho	icebreaker
la rondine marina	la ron-dee-nay ma-ree-na	tern
la roulotte	la roo-lot-tay	caravan
il rovo	eel ro-vo	thornbush
la Russia	la roos-see-a	Russia
la sabbia	la sab-bee-a	sand
le sabbie mobili (f)	lay sab-bee-ay mo-bee-lee	quicksand
i sacchi (m)	ee sack-kee	sacks
il salvagente	eel sal-va-jen-tay	lifebelt
il sampan cinese	eel sam-pan chee-nay-zay	sampan
i sandali	ee san-da-lee	sandals
il sari	eel sa-ree	sari
i sassi	ee sas-see	stones
il sasso	eel sas-so	stone
il sassofono	eel sas-so-fo-no	saxophone
i sassolini	ee sas-so-lee-nee	pebbles
il sassolino	ee sas-so-lee-no	pebble
lo sbarramento	lo zbar-ra-men-to	weir
lo scalatore	lo sca-la-to-ray	climber
la scaletta	la sca-let-ta	steps
lo scaricatore	lo sca-ree-ca-to-ray	docker
gli scarponi da montagna (m)	lyee scar-po-nee da mon-ta-nya	climbing boots
lo scheletro	lo scay-lay-tro	skeleton
gli sci (m)	lyee shee	skis
lo sciale	lo shal-lay	shawl
la scialuppa di salvataggio	la shal-loo-pa dee sal-va-taj-jo	lifeboat
la sciarpa	la shee-ar-pa	scarf
lo scienziato	lo shen-tsee-a-to	scientist
la scimmia	la sheem-mee-a	monkey
lo scimpanze	lo sheem-pan-tsay	chimpanze
la sciovia	la shee-o-vee-a	ski lift
lo scoglio	lo sco-lyee-o	rock
lo scorpione	lo scor-pee-o-nay	scorpion
lo scudo	lo scoo-do	shield
la scure	la scoo-ray	axe

Italian	Pronunciation	English
la sedia a sdraio	la say-dee-a a zdra-yo	deckchair
la sega	la say-ga	saw
il segnale stradale	eel say-nya-lay stra-da-lay	road sign
la sella	la sel-la	saddle
il semaforo	eel say-ma-fo-ro	traffic lights
il serpente	eel ser-pen-tay	snake
la Sfinge	la sfeen-jay	Sphinx
il silofono	eel see-lo-fo-no	xylophone
la slitta	la sleet-ta	sledge
lo smoking	lo smo-keeng	tuxedo
il sombrero	eel som-bray-ro	sombrero
sott'aqua	sot-tack-kwa	underwater
sotto	sot-to	under
sotto il mare	sot-to eel ma-ray	under the sea
il sottomarino	eel sot-to-ma-ree-no	submarine
gli spaghetti (m)	lyee spa-get-tee	spaghetti
gli speroni (m)	lyee spay-ro-nee	spurs
lo spiedino alla brace	lo spee-ay-dee-no al-la bra-chay	shish kebab
la spugna	la spoo-nya	sponge
gli Stati Uniti	lyee sta-tee oo-nee-tee	United States (of America)
la statua	la sta-too-a	statue
La Statua della Libertà	la sta-too-a del-la lee-ber-ta	The Statue of Liberty
la stella marina	la stel-la ma-ree-na	starfish
lo stendardo	lo sten-dar-do	banner
gli stivali (m)	lyee stee-va-lee	boots
Stonehenge	ston-enj	Stonehenge
la strada sopraelevata	la stra-da sop-ra-ay-lay-va-ta	flyover
la strega	la stray-ga	witch
lo struzzo	lo stroot-so	ostrich
il subacqueo	eel soob-ack-kway-o	diver
il Sud America	eel sood a-may-ree-ca	South America
sull'acqua	sool-lack-kwa	on the water
il tabacco	eel ta-back-ko	tobacco
il tacchino	eel tack-kee-no	turkey
il Taj Mahal	eel taj ma-al	Taj Mahal
il tamburello	eel tam-boo-rel-lo	tambourine
il tamburo	eel tam-boo-ro	drum
il tandem	eel tan-dem	tandem
il tapiro	eel ta-pee-ro	tapir
la tartaruga del deserto	la tar-tar-oo-ga del day-zer-to	desert turtle
il tasso	eel tas-so	badger
il tè	eel tay	tea
la tempesta di sabbia	la tem-pes-ta dee sab-bee-a	sandstorm
Il Tempio del Paradiso	eel tem-pee-o del pa-ra-dee-zo	The Temple of Heaven
la tenda	la ten-da	tent
la tenda beduina	la ten-da bay-doo-ee-na	Bedouin tent
la tenda mongola	la ten-da mon-go-la	yurt
il tentacolo	eel ten-ta-co-lo	tentacle
il terremoto	eel ter-ray-mo-to	earthquake
il teschio	eel tes-kee-o	skull
la testuggine gigante	la tes-tooj-jee-nay jee-gan-tay	giant tortoise
la tigre	la tee-gray	tiger
il timpano	eel teem-pa-no	kettle drum
la tonaca del prete	la to-na-ca del pre-tay	cassock
la tonaca della monaca	la to-na-ca del-la mo-na-ca	habit
il topo	eel to-po	mouse, rat
il topo saltatore	eel to-po sal-ta-to-ray	kangaroo rat
la tormenta	la tor-men-ta	blizzard
la Torre di Londra	la tor-ray dee lon-dra	The Tower of London
la Torre Eiffel	la tor-ray eef-fel	The Eiffel Tower
la Torre Pendente di Pisa	la tor-ray pen-den-tay dee pee-za	The Leaning Tower of Pisa
la torta	la tor-ta	cake
il tortino di carne	eel tor-tee-no dee car-nay	meat pie
il tramezzino	eel tra-med-zee-no	sandwich
I trampoli (m)	ee tram-po-lee	stilts
il trattore	eel trat-to-ray	tractor
il trattore da neve	eel trat-to-ray da nay-vay	snowtractor
il treno	eel tray-no	train
il triangolo	eel tree-an-go-lo	triangle
il tricheco	eel tree-kay-co	walrus
la tromba	la trom-ba	trumpet
la tromba d'aria	la trom-ba da-ree-a	tornado
la tromba marina	la trom-ba ma-ree-na	waterspout
il trombone	eel trom-bo-nay	trombone
il tronco	eel tron-co	tree trunk, log
il tronco dell'albero	eel tron-co del-al-bay-ro	tree trunk
la tuba	la too-ba	tuba
il tucano	eel too-ca-no	toucan
i tulipani	ee too-lee-pa-nee	tulips
il tulipano	eel too-lee-pa-no	tulip
il turbante	eel toor-ban-tay	turban
la tuta spaziale	la too-ta spat-see-a-lay	space suit
la tuta sportiva	la too-ta spor-tee-va	tracksuit
l'uistiti (m)	loo-ee-stee-tee	marmoset
l'uncino (m)	loon-chee-no	hook
l'uva (f)	loo-va	grapes
la valanga	la va-lan-ga	avalanche
la vela	la vay-la	sail
il velo mussulmano	eel vay-lo moos-sool-ma-no	yashmak
vestirsi	ves-teer-see	to dress
in viaggio!	een vee-aj-jo	on the move
il vino	eel vee-no	wine
il violino	eel vee-o-lee-no	violin
il violoncello	eel vee-o-lon-chel-lo	cello
la volpe bianca	la vol-pay bee-an-ca	white fox
la volpe del deserto	la vol-pay del day-zer-to	desert fox
il vombato	eel vom-ba-to	wombat
il vulcano	eel vool-ca-no	volcano
il wigwam	eel wig-wam	wigwam
i würster	ee woor-ster	frankfurters
lo zaino	lo dza-ee-no	haversack
la zattera	la dzat-tay-ra	raft
la zebra	la dzeb-ra	zebra
gli zoccoli olandesi (m)	lyee tsock-ko-lee o-lan-day-zee	clogs
lo zucchero	lo tsook-cay-ro	sugar